How To Start An Online Crafting Business: On A Budget

Erin M. Lloyd-Evans, BSBA

ISBN-10: 1492728985
ISBN-13: 978-1492728986

DEDICATION

This book is dedicated to my children Sophia and Noah (who are my joy), my husband of 10 years Tye, my mother Vexie, and my two fur babies Sammie and Gigi. I love all of you :)!!!

CONTENTS

	Acknowledgments	4
1	Finding Your Niche	5-10
2	I Need Supplies and Lots of Them	11-16
	Erin	
3	Choosing A Business Name and Insurance	17-22
4	Domain Registration	23-27
5	Website Set Up	28-32
6	Marketing and Advertising	33-36
7	I Built It But They Are Not Coming, What Now?	37-40
8	Selling Via Other Online Markets and Craft Shows To Supplement Your Income	41-52
9	Resources	53-60
10	About The Author	61

ACKNOWLEDGMENTS

I would like to acknowledge my husband and mother who both encouraged me to write this book. To my husband, thank you for providing me with quiet evenings and weekends by watching our beautiful children. Thank you for being my rock and support when I felt at times that I could not do this. You have always supported me since day one and believed in me and SophiasNaturals.com. From the bottom of my heart thank you Babe :)!!

To my mother, thank you for instilling in me that I could do and become anything that I wanted to be in life. Because of the values that you instilled in me I am now a successful business owner (and soon to be MBA graduate) wife, mother, and now author. You paved the way for me to do well in life and now I am able to share this with my family. I Thank You Mommy!! To all of my aunts, uncles, cousins thank you for pushing me to do well in life and providing me with invaluable life lessons. It is because of all of you that I am the person that I am today.

1 FINDING YOUR NICHE

This sounds easy doesn't it? Find your niche. Essentially it is. Finding your niche is really what you are good at or what you love to do. When starting your online craft business you have to figure this out before you begin. I learned the hard way. I went from figuring that sewing was my niche (because I could sew pretty well) to art work and then to paper crafts. However none of these crafts turned out to be my "it" factor. When choosing your niche you have to figure out what is actually profitable and what you can see yourself potentially doing for the rest of your life.

I happened upon my niche when I was working as a federal employee. I was a young mother, in school and working full-time and I needed a release. I had done tons of research and I came across soap making as a hobby.

I thought that this might be something that I am good at and I began to look for suppliers. The first company that I came across after entering the terms "wholesale, soap, supplies" was www.wholesalesuppliesplus.com. I was able to buy materials in bulk from them to make products, obtain recipes, and ask questions if I had any. What started out as a stress relieving hobby for me ended up becoming a profitable business! The rest is history and after many years and learned lessons my niche "soap" SophiasNaturals.com was born.

So, I bet you are saying now, okay Erin, but how do I find my niche and what I am good at? For trying to find your niche I suggest first doing a generalized Google search to find a list of various crafts that are out there. Examples are: wood work, paper crafting, scrapbooking, sewing, soaping, etc. The list goes on and on.

After you obtain a list I suggest narrowing it down to your top five choices. With your five selections you will begin to research and find out which craft/trade fits you the best. There are many excellent resources to find out how certain things are made such as YouTube and Google. You want to make sure that you are looking for tutorials on how to do the craft from start to finish. At this point you should be ready to shave down your list a bit more (only two or three selections).

With your final selections in tow you have to be ready to

pick the winner soon. At this stage you should be researching to see if there are any online forums and local classes for trade newbie's in your area. Craigslist is often a great site to use for finding local cost friendly craft/trade classes in your area.

You can also do a Google search to see if any local companies hold workshops too. I recommend taking workshop courses for your final two to three niche choices. After you take your courses you will know what you feel you can be good at. Will you be a master at the niche craft after one course? No, probably not but you will know what you are capable of and if you continue at it you will one day become a master at it.

Okay Erin, I have found my niche and am pretty good at

my craft now what? Well this is where you start the testing phase. You make product and you give it to your family and friends and get their opinion on it. If you want to get an honest opinion you can tell them that you purchased the item for them to get a true reaction.

If they really like it start to ask them a couple of questions about it to get good feedback. Such as would they pay for it? how much would they pay for it?, and do they believe that it is a marketable item? Even if you get less than favorable answers from your friends and family do not let this discourage you. Remember you are just starting out and are learning along the way or paying for your experience.

At this point you should be looking for professional organizations (of the craft/trade) that you can join. These organizations are invaluable pools of information as well as guidance for your craft.

With the help of craft online forums I mentioned earlier and the professional organizations you will be hone in on your craft over the next year. I recommend waiting at least two years or more of crafting before you offer your products online. This gives you the needed experience and know how in your craft area. For individuals that are reading this book and already have a craft niche, and experience please continue to the next chapter.

2 I NEED SUPPLIES AND LOTS OF THEM ERIN!!!

Alright I have some experience now I need some budget friendly equipment and supplies without breaking the bank, Erin. Ahh, I am glad you have asked my friend because I like to think of myself as the thrifty queen.

Equipment depending on what niche craft you have chosen can be a bit costly. For example let's look at sewing. To purchase everything brand new you could be looking at least $500.00 or more for a good quality and heavy duty machine. That does not include the material, thread, storage for materials etc.

Now let's look at this same example but buying our items

a bit more cost friendlier or in other words gently used. You can find very nice equipment at local thrift shops or local yard sells for sale. I say check here first because there is the least amount of hassle on your part. You can test the equipment there to make sure that it works and often you can talk the seller into a better deal. Another local option is craigslist or other classified listings such as eBay classifieds.

These places are great to look for crafting equipment because most times individuals are looking to get rid of a bulk of items. I recommend if you are planning to go the craigslist route to take someone with you. Do not plan the pickup trip alone as we all know there are plenty of crazies out here.

I do not want you to think that online classified sites are all bad. I recently was able to make a huge score from a local fellow soap artisan that was going out of business. I got tons of new supplies to use in my business. I recommend though that as a general rule of thumb do not use products that have already been open. Yes folks you want to use the age old

Halloween candy rule for this one. If it is open or unwrapped please chuck it. You also have to be gentle to the individual you are purchasing from. If they are a crafter like you they want to make sure that their supplies are going to a good home. So don't throw away the open products in their face wait until you get home and do it. Also please disinfect everything before you bring it into your workspace area and use it.

Another option for scoring budget friendly supplies is of course the World Wide Web. Ebay.com is a great site to use for getting equipment and supplies on the cheap. One trick that I use for equipment that is gently used (that I really want) I contact the seller directly by asking them if they are willing to do a buy it now for their current price or a couple bucks lower.

This option works well because if your piece of equipment or supplies is being watched by many ebayers you can cut the fat so it speak and save a few bucks in the process. It does not always work with the sellers. Since I have been ebaying I have had three sellers tell me no in the past six years.

Etsy.com which is a place where artisans can sell their

goods in a large marketplace is a gold mine for destashing. Destashing means to get rid of your personal stash of supplies and equipment. To search for destashed items in your craft niche you want to enter the name of your craft (soap, for example) and then the word destash. So it should read "soap destash". Other ways to search on etsy for supplies are craft name and then supplies or supply lot after it. I have scored unique supplies as well as some hard to find items in my craft field.

I will give you a piece of sound advice for searching for supplies on eBay and etsy. You must search on a daily basis in order to find specific items. Fellow crafters are often looking for a lot of the same items as you and if they see it first they will purchase it. As a last resort if you have to pay full price for your supplies please make sure that you are purchasing from a trusted supplier in your craft field. Do not just purchase from any online store. Quite often your professional membership organization will have a listing of trusted suppliers too.

3 CHOOSING A BUSINESS NAME AND INSURANCE

At least two years under your belt of experience, check. Now what do I do? Your next step is to figure out a business name. Business names are a tricky business because you have to make sure that your name is unique and it also represents your brand well. You have to make sure that your business name is unique because you do not want to infringe on another person or company's trademarked information.

Even though your name maybe original and new to you it may not be to others. After you choose your name I recommend running it through the US Patent and Trademark: www.uspto.gov/trademarks. I would also recommend doing a state search to make sure that no one else has an LLC under that name too in your state. That can also be a big mess if two companies in the same state have the same name. Trying to register for tax ids and trying to establish brand identity would be nightmare not to mention potential lawsuits.

Doing these steps will save you a headache in the future. Once you have found a free and clear name you are ready to start on building your brand. Once you choose your name you need to register it first with a domain registration service (which I will go into detail in the next chapter). Then you need to go to every social media website (that is popular out there, i.e. twitter, facebook, instagram, Google plus, vine, pinterest, LinkedIn, etc) and create a business based page. It is very simple to set up business based pages on all of these websites mentioned. You would just register as normal except on facebook which requires you to have facebook page. These facebook pages are linked to a personal facebook account. On these pages you are allowed to assign other page managers and post as an admin at all times even when you are logged in under your personal information.

Your business name is locked in now what? Well I recommend getting your business registered in your state there are three types of businesses which are sole proprietorship, limited liability corporation, and corporation. Sole proprietorships are companies that are run by one individual hence "sole". As a sole proprietorship you have no other individuals that have a stake or share in your company. With a limited liability corporation you have two or more individuals that have shares in the company that share the liability as well.

As a small business starting out you will not have to worry about corporation status unless your business skyrockets overnight. It can happen but there are few success stories like this. If you are running this company by yourself you should register with your state as a sole proprietorship. This costs a couple hundred bucks depending on your state. There are many companies that offer this service online for company registrations but do not go with them because it is a rip off. You can easily go to your local county office and do it yourself and save a few hundred bucks.

After you are registered with your state your next step

should be to register for an employer identification number with the IRS or EIN. You will see companies on the internet that also say that they can get EIN's and charge you. Do not go with those companies you can get an EIN for free with the IRS. You can apply for one online by visiting www.irs.gov and searching for EIN. It takes a few minutes and you are given an EIN based off of your personal tax identification number. This EIN number is totally different from your personal tax identification number so have no worries.

Business name, check, state registration, check, EIN, check, now what? At this point you will begin to feel like everything is starting to come together and you are almost ready to start selling product. You are not ready yet. The most important part of your business is having business insurance. This insurance protects you in the event that someone tries to sue you because of your product or service. There are many companies that offer crafter's insurance and one of the cost friendly options is a company named RLI Insurance. Their website is www.rlicorp.com. They have competitive rates that are based on your location and they cover many different crafts too. If RLI does not have your craft covered you may want to check with your homeowners insurance (for small business coverage) as well.

4 DOMAIN REGISTRATIONS

Well congratulate yourself. You are getting closer to opening up your online shop. Earlier I spoke about registering you domain name. Your domain name is the web address or website that your consumers will enter in order to visit your store. There are many companies that offer domain registration service but I have personally found namecheap.com to be the best.

Go Daddy used to be the major domain registration service but once they decided to support SOPA, companies (including us) decided to jump ship from all companies that supported the SOPA legislation. SOPA was an anti-piracy law that could have a website taken down immediately (without said website owners consent) due to infringements or piracy concerns. Read more about it here: http://en.wikipedia.org/wiki/Stop_Online_Piracy_Act.

Namecheap.com who is anti-SOPA came in and offered low cost domains and hosting. They have packages were you can get a brand new domain name registered, with SSL certificate, WHOIS and website hosting for the entire year for under $100.00. They have complete guides available on their website to assist you with setting up your domain and making it active via their control panel. All of this may sound confusing to you but if you can setup an email account you can register your domain.

It is a simple process that only takes thirty minutes or less.

In general domain registration packages are good in one year intervals. If you have a coupon for namecheap.com (which can be acquired through a quick Google search) you will save more money if you register for more years.

After you setup your control panel you want to set up your SSL certificate on your panel and your email account for your customer service account. Your SSL certificate will allow consumers to make purchase on your website securely. When they enter the "my account" section of your e-store this certificate will show via tiny green lock pad in the web browser. When it is a red lock pad there it means that your SSL certificate has expired and needs to be renewed.

Regarding your customer service email address, please

keep it professional. Do not give your shop an email name such as babyone@yourstorename.com. Would you want to purchase from someone that had a name like this for email? I would not because I would wonder if they were a legit company or not.

You do not want consumers to guess about your company or brand because you only have one chance for them to like your company and continue or to run in the opposite direction and never look back. Use a generalized email such as firstname@yourstorename.com or support or customerservice instead of firstname.

I did not mention this earlier but as we are on the email topic (which is a form of contact) I thought I should mention it. Please get a Google voice phone number for your company. They are free and easy to setup with your gmail.com account. Consumers want to feel that they can get in contact with someone. Having a number allows them to feel that they can contact you another way besides email. With Google voice you can set it up so that it rings to your home phone, cell phone or voicemail. With voicemail all messages are recorded and transcribed with Google voice. So even if you miss a call you can still receive an email with the message and immediately call the customer back.

5 WEBSITE SETUP

Setting a website up and designing it a few years ago would have cost the average small business owner on the cheap end $500.00. Today though, more programmers are building open-source or free scripts. When I first started my online company in 2009 I had to read hours of research and teach myself HTML. Yes I am a self taught webmaster. If you are a master a Microsoft office you can easily learn html too. A couple of bits of code here and there but essentially its Microsoft word pad in the body of the words.

When I taught myself HTML I had to hand code in my shopping cart script using the PayPal script. It was a very nice looking website but updating it was a nightmare. It was horrible because I had to manually upload pictures to my domain and then manually go back and change the HTML or PHP to match that item. I would spend hours, almost full days in just updating the website and trying to make it useable. My biggest fear was that a customer might visit my shop and see that I was tinkering around and would think that we were not legit.

The last straw for me was one weekend when I spent that entire time updating our website. I said (to myself) enough was enough and I began to hunt for a shopping cart script that was free on Google. There were many shopping cart scripts that were just what we needed but they were custom built, or they wanted a large up front setup fee, and a crazy monthly maintenance fee. When it seemed like I had lost all hope on finding a free shopping cart script I came across a link for an OpenCart.com. I figured it was a bust like the others before it but when I clicked on it I found out that it was open-source aka free. I felt like my prayers had been answered.

OpenCart came with a complete script that managed products, inventory, design and feel too. It had options for integration with other software/scripts on the market and most of all it was all free. Did I mention that??? LOL :). Seriously, after reading through their easy directions I was able to get my new shop up and running within 30 minutes or less.

I was also able to begin adding new products to the shop

once live. They provided demo store information (that could later be deleted by you) to show you how to enter products. This script also has built in payment software too. I recommend that as a new online seller you use your PayPal account (www.paypal.com) to accept payments on your website.

It is free (no monthly cost but there is still a per transaction charge) and you can immediately purchase postage through them using USPS or UPS as your shipping providers. Funds from sales are easily deposited into your bank account with three business days (maybe longer depending on your bank).

Once your store is setup with OpenCart you will notice

the demo store logo is still there. You may say to yourself, how can I get a nice logo for cheap? My answer to you would be to use three options. The first is to design a logo yourself using a free software program website such as www.fotoflexer.com.

Option two is to visit www.fiverr.com and go to design services. You can get any work done from this website for just five bucks!! The final option which can be the most expensive is having a pre-made or custom logo made from artisans on etsy or other logo service companies.

6 MARKETING AND ADVERTISING

Your shop is all setup pretty and ready for sales, Now What? This is the portion where you may actually have to spend a little more money to make a little more money. There are many forms of free advertising such as craigslist advertisements, eBay classifieds, listing your company in the online yellow pages, social media and adding your website to the major search engines. However doing just this alone will not yield in large profitable results.

As a small business you have to network. One way is through donations. If you can donate some of your product for certain events or giveaways you will gain some new customers. One great company that is wonderful for getting your brand our there is www.samplervillage.com. They have many active subscribers for their monthly sampler village subscription boxes. Essentially companies such as yours provide sample products (minimum 25) to sampler village and they include them in their monthly boxes for their customers. You receive tons of exposure and advertising for your samples that you provide not to mention networking opportunities with other artisans.

You can also check local events in your area to see if they are accepting donations from sponsors for events too. Please make sure that any donations that you do provide are well packaged and contain your website contact information. Remember that well labeled pretty packaging will catch the eye quicker. Other options are hosting giveaways on your website but you still have to have a steady stream of visitors in order for this option to work.

The biggest form of advertising is through a method called Google ad words. With Google ad words you pick keywords, build a campaign, and set how much you would like to pay per day for advertising across the web Based upon the keywords you chose and you daily budget for your brand will determine how well you do in sales. Of course when figuring out your final profit you have to include your cost of advertising. Your final profit would be the amount of sales less what you paid for operating expenses and advertising/marketing expenses.

Another form of Google ad word like advertising is

through facebook. Facebook offers ads now which guarantee a certain amount of likes based upon your daily advertising budget. While facebook ads is similar to Google ad words in concept you can have days that go by where you do not receive any likes and still are required to pay for impressions. To me they did not seem viable for a smaller business such as myself. I do think that they are good advertising service but I feel that if I am paying I should at least be getting more likes per day.

7 I BUILT IT BUT THEY ARE NOT COMING, NOW WHAT?

I say, slow down young grasshopper. You must have patience. We are in the technology age and years ago before the dot.com crash new online companies did great. Companies back then did better in sales simply because there were not many companies that were online yet. Many companies were still selling via mail or phone order. Fast forward to today and everyone has a website. Even your local elementary school has a website now.

It takes time to build a brand and it takes even more time for your website to show up in search engines and in advertising campaigns. Customers are not just going to purchase from you because you have a cool website, awesome products and the prices are just right. As I type this I chuckle a bit because I should have been listening to my own advice when I started out. When you build something from the ground up and you know that it is special you want everyone to experience that. I get it and can relate to you the most.

It used to bother me so much that I spent so much time making products, building my website, using social media and still not receiving sales online. You see so many successful companies in your craft niche that are doing well, receiving sells and wonder what is wrong with me and my brand. I will answer and tell you that there is nothing wrong with you or your craft. The only thing that your competitor has as their advantage is time in the field and the consumer base.

Do not allow yourself to get discouraged. You have to build up your customer base, customer service and get yourself recognized as a newbie in the craft niche (that is planning to stay). Being consistent in everything that you do will help people to remember you. It can be your daily posts to facebook, twitter or your blog that show a customer or a company that you are worth visiting or mentioning.

Another tool which is really great for getting new customers and letting people know what you and your company are about is youtube.com. YouTube is excellent for showing potential consumers how you make your product or how to use your product. If you are going to use

YouTube as a way to drum up new business please remember to make videos in well lit areas and use a camera tripod so that your video does not move around all crazy.

Alright we are going to pull up our bootstraps now (yes I am talking to you) and move on along to the next chapter. Pity parties are never fun as you are always the only person throwing it and attending it. So no more feeling sorry for yourself!! It is time to configure a plan of action to get those customers coming in. Get creative and remember to have fun in the process.

8 SELLING VIA OTHER ONLINE MARKETS AND CRAFT SHOWS TO SUPPLEMENT YOUR INCOME

So we are ready to be ultimate sellers now aren't we? There are many ways to sell your crafts online but you must choose wisely. You do not want to have your products in every online market place and your shop because it can get confusing and time consuming (because there is no software or script currently that allows all of the different markets to talk to one another).

This can be a nightmare regarding inventory upkeep and overselling products that may not be in stock. For this reason I have decided to give you my tried and true companies to use when selling your products.

The first company is ebay.com. Yes ebay.com is overly saturated with craft providers but quite often competitor products can be inferior (in presentation or quality), cost more, or are coming from overseas. These are all things that customers do not want. When consumers shop on eBay they are looking for the best price on specific goods or similar goods.

Your product can fall in either one of these categories and you can get new customers. Now eBay does charge twice. Once to list and they receive a percentage of the final sale but at least you are making a sale versus the product sitting on the shelf and collecting dust. You can also accept payment via PayPal from your consumers too.

The second company is etsy.com. Etsy is designed solely for artisans. Consumers visit this website to find unique handmade items that are made with love. The market here is heavy for all artisans and they charge twice as well too. They also charge for your etsy shop to be featured in search ads which can range from a few dollars per week up to a couple hundred.

In terms of fees they are cheaper than eBay but eBay has a larger audience. Etsy also has many unique marketing tools which can be used across the web such as their embeddable code for shops and their ability to offer consumers coupons. PayPal or credit cards are the payment processors for etsy as well.

The third company which is great for getting your brand out is opensky.com. They have recently opened up a merchant portal which allows artisans to sell their products to millions of consumers every day. They do not charge you a listing fee but they do charge you a percentage of the final sale and for credit card processing.

From what I gather the more you agree to participate in their special offerings for customers the better your shop gets advertised (meaning front page exposure) and more money. To get the opportunity to sell on opensky is a bit of a pain in the beginning especially if you do not have any followers, friends, or fans on social media. They require you to send at least 20 people to opensky in order for them to approve your store for sales and for the public to be able to see it. It sounds crazed I know but it does pay off in the long run. We did it and sales have been steady on opensky.com.

Another method for getting sales is through craft shows or trade shows. There are many places to search for shows such as craigslist under community or events, etsy's community groups for your local area, and Google.

There are websites such as just to name a few:

www.festivalnet.com

www.artsandcraftshows-usa.com

www.artscraftsshowbusiness.com

I also would like to offer some advice I learned along the

way. Start small and get a feel for trade/craft shows. If you are just starting out and your table presentation is not the best do not start off with the more expensive shows. The expensive shows ($150 and up) have many rules and regulations. Not to mention that most often they are judged by a jury.

Meaning that you will have to provide professional pictures of your setup and all of your business information before you can submit your final payment. There is normally an upfront application fee (which is non-refundable if you are chosen or not) and the event fee (which is normally $150 or more).

Purchasing items for your booth can be very expensive.

Folding tables can run about $50.00 to $75.00, floor length table covers can run $45-$50 per table, table displays can run $45-90 per display, a good 10x10 folding tent with weights ($250.00), banners and signs another couple hundred.

I am not trying to discourage anyone from doing a larger show but there are a lot of startup costs involved and there is always the chance that you may not make your table money back. Table money refers to the money spent to reserve your spot at the show. If you are looking for trade show items I suggest again craigslist, eBay, etsy, and Amazon for obtaining low cost equipment.

If you have found your first craft show and you feel like it is a good fit please read my advice on actual craft shows here:

Here are few things that we have learned about being a successful vendor.

1) Equipment- Always, Always, Always do a pre-setup with your table and equipment prior to arriving at your event. You need to do this to make sure that everything is working. Nothing is more time consuming for you to arrive at your event and having to run around to look for replacement equipment.

2) Arrival Time- Always show up earlier than your assigned set up time. This is a great tip because you can normally get first dips on the best spot. Another reason is because you have more time to work out how you want your display setup to look and feel.

3) Table Setup- Until recently, I always felt that you should use the U setup with your tables because it gives your tent a home like feel. It was not until I actually set everything up as in step one that I realized this would not work. While a U shaped table display would be nice and give a nice feel it would only feel that way to you. Customers do not want to feel trapped especially if they are just walking by.

With having your table display facing the customers you are able to allow them shop and browse your items without feeling confined. With our setup we wanted to make sure that we could catch consumers from both angles and it was a success. The only thing that I would change in the future would be to add another 1x10 banner so that our shop sign is displayed clearly on both sides (I had a couple older folks think that I was selling salt water taffies and fudge because of the colors and size of our soaps, LOL :)).

4) Table Decor- When decorating your table you should try to keep displays cost friendly but also make them look neat and make them relate to your theme. Also always have floor length table covers. It does not look good to customers when they can see all of your what nots and inventory under the table.

5) Your Register- Make sure that you have plenty of change as well as the ability to accept credit cards. Most companies offer free credit card terminal swipes (that can be used with your smart phone) with low cost transaction fees.

Some companies are GoPayment by Intuit, PayPal, Square, and Bank of America. I have all of them except for PayPal and I honestly recommend GoPayment because they have more ability to personalize receipts which the other two do not.

5) Open For Business- Always greet every customer that even may glance your way. If a customer feels welcomed enough they will come over. There is no need to yell, shout or pressure customers into buying your products. When a customer comes over to your booth stand up and greet them (if you are sitting) and make small talk by asking them how they are doing today. Make sure to answer all of their questions if any. Also even if a customer does or does not purchase make sure to thank them for their time.

6) Talking with Other Vendors- You should always make time to talk to and meet with other vendors. It helps to build good relationships as well as other potential networking opportunities.

Our setup processes and methods will only continue over time and yours will too. Still waiting I see! GET OUT THERE AND SELL! ☺ I believe in you and so should you!!!

WEBSITE RESOURCES LISTED IN THIS BOOK:

www.artsandcraftshows-usa.com –

Is a complete website listing of craft shows across the US by date.

www.artscraftsshowbusiness.com-

Is a complete website listing of craft shows across the US by date.

www.amazon.com-

It is a large online marketplace and is a great source for finding crafting equipment and supplies for you business.

www.etsy.com-

Is an online market place made solely for artisans selling handcrafted and vintage items. This is not only a great place to sell your product but it is also a great place to find new and used crafting equipment as well.

www.ebay.com-

Is the largest online auction marketplace for used and new items. This is not only a great place to sell your product but it is also a great place to find new and used crafting equipment as well.

www.facebook.com-

Is a social media website that allows you to connect with family, friends, and customers all in one place. You are allowed to post statuses, pictures, links and more.

www.festivalnet.com-

Is a complete website listing of craft shows across the US by date.

www.fotoflexer.com-

Is a totally free online photo editing software. With this software you can create logos, banners, and more.

www.fiverr.com-

Is a low cost graphic design task website. Here all graphic design jobs start at just $5.00. Depending on what you want additional fees may apply. The general turnaround time for purchased projects is one to three business days.

www.gmail.com-

It is a free email account provider website. Once you sign up for a free account you are able to use this same account to create a Google voice number, to setup your Google ad words account, and to set up your YouTube account. Everything will be linked to the one email account that you choose and sign up is super easy.

www.google.com/adwords-

It is the largest online advertiser for creating promotional (online) campaigns for your business.

www.instagram.com-

It is a social media photo based website that allows you to share photos of your products with your followers and receive their comments and suggestions in real-time.

www.linkedin.com-

Is the biggest professional social media networking site. This is a great tool as you are able to network with other companies as well as potential wholesalers.

www.namecheap.com-

Is the best online domain registrar and hosting provider around. You are able to receive excellent and consistent service for a fair price.

www.opencart.com-

It is an open source (free) shopping cart software that can be integrated with multiple scripts.

www.opensky.com-

It is a newer online marketplace that is designed around the use of social media. Customers are allowed to share, like, recommend and love products. All of these options result in higher exposure for your business.

www.paypal.com-

Is the largest and most trusted online payment processor for sending and receiving e-payments.

www.pinterest.com-

It is a social media photo based website where you can share and like pictures.

www.rlicorp.com-

The most cost friendliest provider of crafter/artisan insurance on the web.

www.samplervillage.com-

Is a company that is designed to help you promote your goods through the donation of samples from you.

www.SophiasNaturals.com-

This is my company!! We are a natural soap and bath company that focuses on selling items that are free from parabens and sulfates.

www.twitter.com-

Is a social media website that allows you to deliver quick notes, links, and photos to your followers.

www.vine.com-

Is a social media website in which you can take clips of video and make a short looping video. This is really cool for those that can show how they do certain crafts.

www.wholesalesuppliesplus.com-

Is one of largest suppliers of wholesale soap and bath products on the web. They are one of my favorite companies for my own supplies.

www.youtube.com-

Is a video based social media website that allows you to upload videos on almost any subject for free.

ABOUT THE AUTHOR

Erin M. Lloyd-Evans got her first taste of the entrepreneurial spirit at the young age of 14. She was chosen to be a member of the University of Pennsylvania's "Young Entrepreneur Summer Program". As a inter city youth this program gave her the knowledge of starting and operating a successful business as an entrepreneur.

Mrs. Lloyd-Evans is currently married with two children and lives in Georgia. She is the owner of SophiasNaturals.com which is an online soap and bath product shop that sells natural products free from parabens and sulfates. This company was started in 2009 as a hobby but quickly grew into a profitable business. Mrs. Evans obtained her associates and bachelor's degrees in business administration and she is currently in school to obtain her MBA.

6341107R00036

Printed in Great Britain
by Amazon.co.uk, Ltd.,
Marston Gate.